IF IT IS TO BE

Written by Dr. Terry J. Flowers

Illustrated by Emmanuel Gillespie

Inspired Forever Books
Dallas, Texas

If It Is To Be
Copyright © 2025 Dr. Terry J. Flowers

All rights reserved, including the right of reproduction in whole or in part in any form without prior written permission, except in the case of brief quotations embodied in critical reviews and certain other noncommercial uses permitted by copyright law.

Inspired Forever Books
Dallas, Texas
(888) 403-2727
Words With Lasting Impact™
https://inspiredforeverbooks.com

Paperback ISBN 13: 978-1-948903-98-1
Library of Congress Number: 2025920857
Printed in the United States of America

Illustrations by Emmanuel Gillespie

Title consultant Iv Amenti

Life's circumstances are inseparable from an undeniable truth: while there are many reasons behind our challenges, we must not allow them to transform into excuses. This book is dedicated to those who embrace that belief........ MANY REASONS BUT NO EXCUSES. Its words and images are offered to inspire both youth and adults to rise above obstacles, resist excuses, and claim their God-given power and responsibility to society.

If It Is To Be honors the collective influence that blesses every student of St. Philip's School and Community Center in Dallas, Texas. It stands as one of many efforts to share with others the faith, resilience, and strong foundation our students receive.

TGBTG… To God Be the Glory

Look at me.

I am more than what you see.

Destiny is mine!

If it is to be, it's up to me.

Society will condemn,
but only I determine my path.

My people have suffered and died
for my chance to read and do math.

Just as sacrifices were made
to make my future bright...

...it is my responsibility to do things that are right.

I must start today to pave the way.

The community and the world
need my contributions.

In success, I will not stray.

The bias, the rumors, nor the stereotypes will hinder my growth.

I claim dignity and prosperity.

My God promises both.

Look at me!

I am sharp, empowered, talented and proud without limit.

I will use my education to
explore new heights.

The sky is the limit, if I just put my mind in it.

When I say, "stick it out,"
I don't mean a hand.

I will persevere to play my role
in God's omniscient plan.

I will live by "put ups, not put downs" for my sister and my brother.

I care for you; I respect you.

If I don't, why should another?

Success is my right - failure my option.
I have the voice.

The consequences I will accept,
for I made the choice.

Look at me!

Great things lie ahead.

Judge me not by what you've been told, but by what's in my head.

Photo Credit: Tia Starghill

Dr. Terry J. Flowers serves as The Perot Family Headmaster of St. Philip's School and Community Center, where he started in service as principal in 1983. Dr. Flowers grew up in Chicago's South Side, ultimately finding a calling to work with young children. The titles of his three master's degrees attest to his commitment to education: Early Childhood Education (University of Northern Iowa), Curriculum and Instruction, and Educational Administration (Columbia University). He also completed a doctorate in Education at the Teacher's College of Columbia University in 1995.

His experiences as an educator in tough urban communities shaped his belief in the need for holistic efforts to address the erosion of inner-city neighborhoods. Dr. Flowers's leadership led to the establishment of a curriculum for St. Philip's that emphasizes academic excellence, a positive self-image, and a faith-based focus for life. Alongside the strong academic program is a multi-faceted community center offering a wealth of social services and community development activities that are crucial to the revitalization of the surrounding neighborhood in which St. Philip's resides. The broad-based approach has established St. Philips's as a model for inner-city schools.

The St. Philip's Creed, a declaration that inspires and affirms the limitless potential of children and youth, was authored by Dr. Flowers in 1984. This foundational creed was first incorporated into his debut children's book, *Destiny Is Mine!* published in 2022. He subsequently released *Put Me Down and Let Me Walk!* in 2023, followed by *The Pink Tornado* and *Turn Your Mirror into a Window* in 2024, further advancing his commitment to empowering young minds through literature.

https://www.stphilips1600.org

www.ingramcontent.com/pod-product-compliance
Lightning Source LLC
Chambersburg PA
CBHW060820090426
42738CB00002B/58